C000036640

Skills Builders

Times Tables

7, 9, 11 AND 12

Hilary Koll and Steve Mills

RISING ★ STARS

PLEASE NOTE: THIS BOOK MAY NOT BE PHOTOCOPIED OR REPRODUCED AND WE APPRECIATE YOUR HELP IN PROTECTING OUR COPYRIGHT.

Rising Stars UK Ltd, 7 Hatchers Mews, Bermondsey Street, London SE1 3GS
www.risingstars-uk.com

Every effort has been made to trace copyright holders and obtain their permission for the use of copyright materials. The publishers will gladly receive information enabling them to rectify any error or omission in subsequent editions.

All facts are correct at time of going to press.

Published 2013
Text, design and layout © 2013 Rising Stars UK Ltd

Project manager: Dawn Booth
Editorial: Roanne Charles
Proofreader: Jane Jackson
Design: Words & Pictures Ltd, London
Cover design: Amina Dudhia

All rights reserved. No part of this publication may be reproduced, stored in a retrieval system, or transmitted, in any form by any means, electronic, mechanical, photocopying, recording or otherwise, without prior permission of Rising Stars.

British Library Cataloguing-in-Publication Data
A CIP record for this book is available from the British Library.

ISBN: 978-0-85769-688-5
Printed in Singapore by Craft Print International

7, 9, 11
AND
12

Contents

How to use this book

What we have included:

- Each unit covers aspects of the multiplication and division facts related to the 7, 9, 11 and 12 times tables.

- Each unit provides opportunity to practise recalling the number facts in and out of order. You can time yourself to see how you are progressing.

- We have included questions that involve a range of mathematical vocabulary, such as product, shared between, divided by, multiple and so on.

- There are three sections of word problems to ensure that you can use your times tables and division facts in many different contexts.

- All answers are included so you can check your progress.

1 Some units begin with a useful tip to help you work out answers to the questions more quickly.

2 **Test 1** involves answering the facts from the times table, usually presented in order. This helps you to see what the unit is about and what you must memorise.

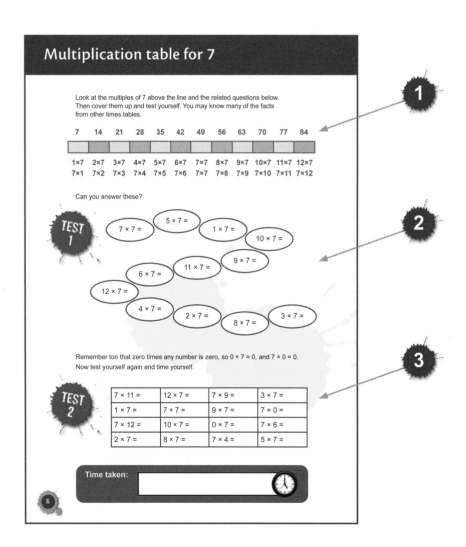

How to use this book

3   **Test 2** gives similar questions but usually in a different order to make sure you learn them in any order. You can also time yourself to see how quickly you can answer them.

4   **Warming up** – This section is based on the same number facts as the tests but are presented in words, using mathematical language you should know.

5   **Getting hotter** – This section involves word problems. You'll need to use the facts you are learning to answer them. Read them very carefully.

6   **Burn it up** – This section has even more challenging questions and problems. You'll need to think very carefully and read each question several times to make sure you reach the correct answer.

7   **How did I do?** This gives you a chance to show how confident you feel about the number facts and to say how well you think you are doing.

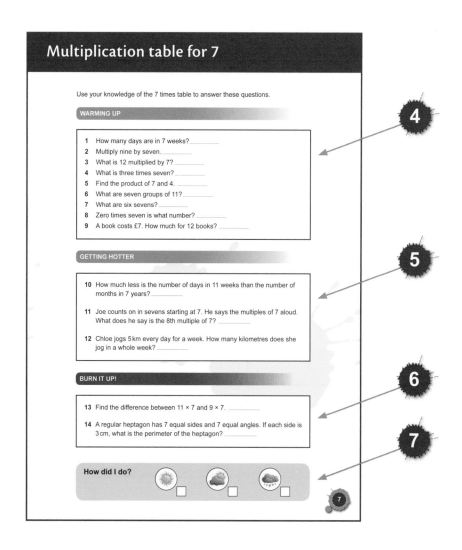

Multiplication table for 7

Use your knowledge of the 7 times table to answer these questions.

WARMING UP   **4**

1. How many days are in 7 weeks? _____
2. Multiply nine by seven. _____
3. What is 12 multiplied by 7? _____
4. What is three times seven? _____
5. Find the product of 7 and 4. _____
6. What are seven groups of 11? _____
7. What are six sevens? _____
8. Zero times seven is what number? _____
9. A book costs £7. How much for 12 books? _____

GETTING HOTTER   **5**

10. How much less is the number of days in 11 weeks than the number of months in 7 years? _____

11. Joe counts on in sevens starting at 7. He says the multiples of 7 aloud. What does he say is the 8th multiple of 7? _____

12. Chloe jogs 5 km every day for a week. How many kilometres does she jog in a whole week? _____

BURN IT UP!   **6**

13. Find the difference between 11 × 7 and 9 × 7. _____

14. A regular heptagon has 7 equal sides and 7 equal angles. If each side is 3 cm, what is the perimeter of the heptagon? _____

7

How did I do?   ☐ ☐ ☐

7

Multiplication table for 7

Look at the multiples of 7 above the line and the related questions below. Then cover them up and test yourself. You may know many of the facts from other times tables.

7	14	21	28	35	42	49	56	63	70	77	84

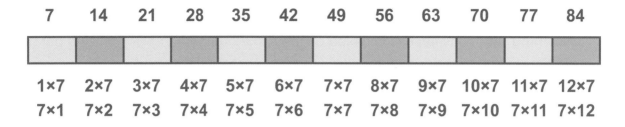

| 1×7 | 2×7 | 3×7 | 4×7 | 5×7 | 6×7 | 7×7 | 8×7 | 9×7 | 10×7 | 11×7 | 12×7 |
| 7×1 | 7×2 | 7×3 | 7×4 | 7×5 | 7×6 | 7×7 | 7×8 | 7×9 | 7×10 | 7×11 | 7×12 |

Can you answer these?

TEST 1

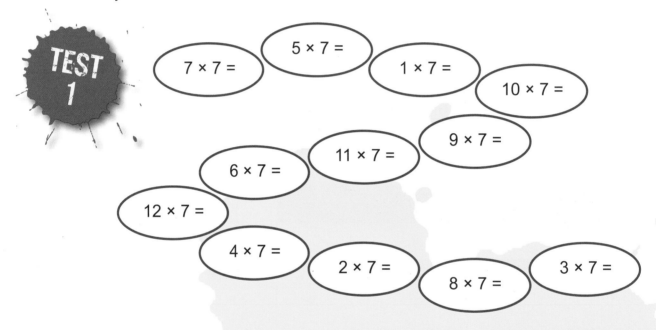

5 × 7 =

7 × 7 =

1 × 7 =

10 × 7 =

9 × 7 =

11 × 7 =

6 × 7 =

12 × 7 =

4 × 7 =

2 × 7 =

8 × 7 =

3 × 7 =

Remember too that zero times any number is zero, so 0 × 7 = 0, and 7 × 0 = 0.

Now test yourself again and time yourself.

TEST 2

7 × 11 =	12 × 7 =	7 × 9 =	3 × 7 =
1 × 7 =	7 × 7 =	9 × 7 =	7 × 0 =
7 × 12 =	10 × 7 =	0 × 7 =	7 × 6 =
2 × 7 =	8 × 7 =	7 × 4 =	5 × 7 =

Time taken:

Multiplication table for 7

Use your knowledge of the 7 times table to answer these questions.

WARMING UP

1   How many days are in 7 weeks?

2   Multiply nine by seven.

3   What is 12 multiplied by 7?

4   What is three times seven?

5   Find the product of 7 and 4.

6   What are seven groups of 11?

7   What are six sevens?

8   Zero times seven is what number?

9   A book costs £7. How much for 12 books?

GETTING HOTTER

10 How much less is the number of days in 11 weeks than the number of months in 7 years?

11 Joe counts on in sevens starting at 7. He says the multiples of 7 aloud. What does he say is the 8th multiple of 7?

12 Chloe jogs 5 km every day for a week. How many kilometres does she jog in a whole week?

BURN IT UP!

13 Find the difference between 11 × 7 and 9 × 7.

14 A regular heptagon has 7 equal sides and 7 equal angles. If each side is 3 cm, what is the perimeter of the heptagon?

How did I do?

Division facts for 7

Look at the division facts below, cover them up, then test yourself.

0 ÷ 7 = 0
7 ÷ 7 = 1
14 ÷ 7 = 2
21 ÷ 7 = 3
28 ÷ 7 = 4
35 ÷ 7 = 5
42 ÷ 7 = 6
49 ÷ 7 = 7
56 ÷ 7 = 8
63 ÷ 7 = 9
70 ÷ 7 = 10
77 ÷ 7 = 11
84 ÷ 7 = 12

TEST 1

0 ÷ 7 =
7 ÷ 7 =
14 ÷ 7 =
21 ÷ 7 =
28 ÷ 7 =
35 ÷ 7 =
42 ÷ 7 =
49 ÷ 7 =
56 ÷ 7 =
63 ÷ 7 =
70 ÷ 7 =
77 ÷ 7 =
84 ÷ 7 =

There are 7 days in each week. Find out how many weeks there are in each number of days by dividing by 7. Time yourself.

TEST 2

49 days = weeks	35 days = weeks	77 days = weeks
63 days = weeks	14 days = weeks	7 days = weeks
21 days = weeks	70 days = weeks	84 days = weeks
56 days = weeks	42 days = weeks	28 days = weeks

Time taken:

Division facts for 7

Use your knowledge of the division facts for the 7 times table to answer these questions.

WARMING UP

1   How many £7 magazines can you buy with £42? ⋯⋯⋯⋯⋯⋯

2   What is zero divided by 7? ⋯⋯⋯⋯⋯⋯

3   Divide 35 by 7. ⋯⋯⋯⋯⋯⋯

4   What is 49 divided by 7? ⋯⋯⋯⋯⋯⋯

5   How many sevens in 28? ⋯⋯⋯⋯⋯⋯

6   How many sevens in seventy? ⋯⋯⋯⋯⋯⋯

7   How many groups of 7 are in 77? ⋯⋯⋯⋯⋯⋯

8   What is the remainder if 84 is divided by 7? ⋯⋯⋯⋯⋯⋯

GETTING HOTTER

9   The entrance fee to a theme park is £7 each. There is a £5 discount taken from the total if 6 or more tickets are bought together. How much would a group of 8 people pay? ⋯⋯⋯⋯⋯⋯

10   When Jacob was two years old, his dad weighed seven times as much as him. If Jacob weighed 12 kg, how much did his dad weigh? ⋯⋯⋯⋯⋯⋯

BURN IT UP!

11   A secret number is multiplied by 7. The answer is 14 greater than the answer to 49 ÷ 7. What is the secret number? ⋯⋯⋯⋯⋯⋯

12   True or false? Dividing an even number by 7 always gives an even answer. ⋯⋯⋯⋯⋯⋯

13   True or false? Dividing an odd multiple of 7 by 7 always gives an odd answer. ⋯⋯⋯⋯⋯⋯

How did I do?

 ☐   ☐   ☐

Multiplication table for 9

The digits of the answers to the 9 times table always add up to 9 (or 18, which makes 9 when the digits are added again).

Look at the patterns, then cover them and answer the questions.

TEST 1

1 × 9 = 9		1 × 9 =
2 × 9 = 18	→ 1 + 8 = 9	2 × 9 =
3 × 9 = 27	→ 2 + 7 = 9	3 × 9 =
4 × 9 = 36	→ 3 + 6 = 9	4 × 9 =
5 × 9 = 45	→ 4 + 5 = 9	5 × 9 =
6 × 9 = 54	→ 5 + 4 = 9	6 × 9 =
7 × 9 = 63	→ 6 + 3 = 9	7 × 9 =
8 × 9 = 72	→ 7 + 2 = 9	8 × 9 =
9 × 9 = 81	→ 8 + 1 = 9	9 × 9 =
10 × 9 = 90	→ 9 + 0 = 9	10 × 9 =
11 × 9 = 99	→ 9 + 9 = 18 → 1 + 8 = 9	11 × 9 =
12 × 9 = 108	→ 1 + 0 + 8 = 9	12 × 9 =

Now answer these questions as quickly as you can. Time yourself. Remember, 9 × 11 has the same answer as 11 × 9, and so on.

TEST 2

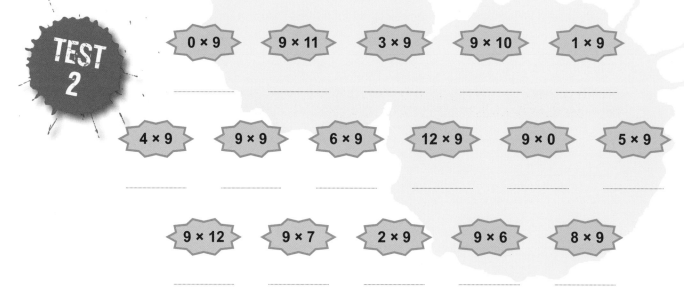

0 × 9   9 × 11   3 × 9   9 × 10   1 × 9

4 × 9   9 × 9   6 × 9   12 × 9   9 × 0   5 × 9

9 × 12   9 × 7   2 × 9   9 × 6   8 × 9

Remember that the digits of the answers to the 9 times table add up to 9 or 18 so use this to help you check your answers.

Time taken:

Multiplication table for 9

1   Multiply 6 by 9. ⎯⎯⎯⎯

2   One-ninth of a number is 2. What is the number? ⎯⎯⎯⎯

3   How much are nine 10p coins worth? ⎯⎯⎯⎯

4   What is the eighth multiple of 9? ⎯⎯⎯⎯

5   What is nine multiplied by seven? ⎯⎯⎯⎯

6   Find the product of 9 and 12. ⎯⎯⎯⎯

7   How much are nine 5 kg weights? ⎯⎯⎯⎯

8   How many sides are there on nine squares? ⎯⎯⎯⎯

9   What are eleven lots of nine? ⎯⎯⎯⎯

GETTING HOTTER

10 A recipe says to use 9 olives per person. When making the recipe for nine people, how many olives from a jar of 100 would you have left over? ⎯⎯⎯⎯

11 Javed uses a scientific formula that says to multiply the mass of an object by 9 to find the force. What number shows the force if the mass of the object is 4 kg? ⎯⎯⎯⎯

12 A rectangle has a length of 9 cm and a width of 7 cm. What is its area?

    ⎯⎯⎯⎯

BURN IT UP!

13 Multiply these teen numbers by 9, using partitioning. One has been done.

    (15)   (13)   (19)   (16)

    10   5   10   3   10   9
    90   45
       135

14 Some chairs are arranged into 9 rows. Each row has 8 chairs. 67 people sit in the chairs. How many empty seats are there? ⎯⎯⎯⎯

How did I do?

Division facts for 9

Remember that division is the inverse of multiplication, so if you know 11 × 9 = 99, then you know that 99 ÷ 9 = 11. Test yourself here.

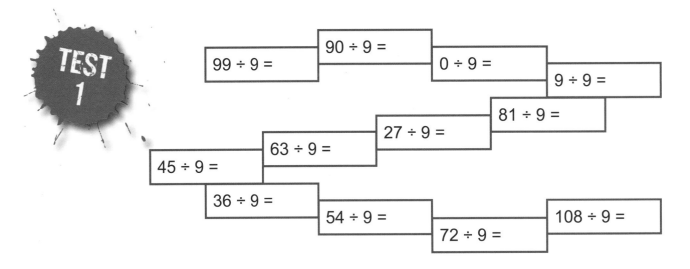

90 ÷ 9 =

99 ÷ 9 =

0 ÷ 9 =

9 ÷ 9 =

81 ÷ 9 =

27 ÷ 9 =

63 ÷ 9 =

45 ÷ 9 =

36 ÷ 9 =

54 ÷ 9 =

108 ÷ 9 =

72 ÷ 9 =

Now divide each of these numbers by 9 as quickly as you can. Time yourself.

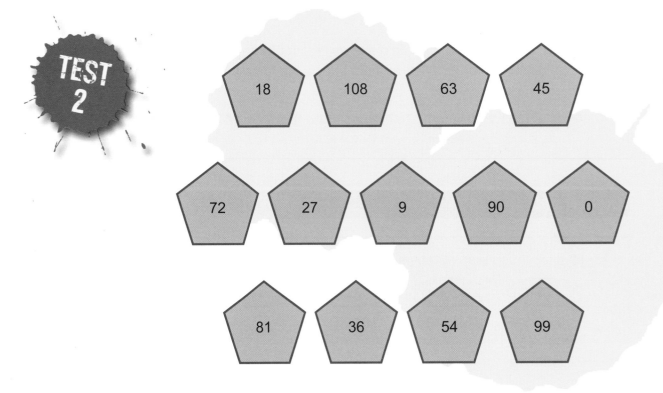

18   108   63   45

72   27   9   90   0

81   36   54   99

Time taken:

12

Division facts for 9

Can you answer these questions using what you know about dividing by 9?

WARMING UP

1   How many wholes are 27 ninths? ....

2   Share 72 grapes between nine. ....

3   Divide 81 by 9 and then divide the answer by 9. ....

4   Nine times a number is 63. What is the number? ....

5   How many nines in thirty-six? ....

6   There are 99 people. They are put into nine equal teams. How many are in each team? ....

7   What is 54 divided by 9? ....

8   How many 9p sweets can you buy with £1.08? ....

GETTING HOTTER

9   There are 9 slices of ham in each pack. In the school kitchen, the cooks have 72 slices of ham. How many packs do they have? ....

10 Tickets for the cinema cost £9 each. What is the largest number of tickets Jack can buy with £100, and how much change will he get? ....

BURN IT UP!

11 Find the difference between one-ninth of 108 and one-ninth of 45. ....

12 What is the remainder when 40 is divided by 9? ....

13 A van uses 1 litre of petrol to travel 9 kilometres. How many litres will it take to travel 81 kilometres, and how much will this cost if petrol is 70p per litre? ....

How did I do?

 ☐   ☐   ☐

Multiplication table for 11

Look at the table below. Notice that for all single-digit numbers multiplied by 11 the answer is that digit written twice, for example: 6 × 11 = 66, 8 × 11 = 88. Now cover the table and test yourself.

0 × 11 = 0
1 × 11 = 11
2 × 11 = 22
3 × 11 = 33
4 × 11 = 44
5 × 11 = 55
6 × 11 = 66
7 × 11 = 77
8 × 11 = 88
9 × 11 = 99
10 × 11 = 110
11 × 11 = 121
12 × 11 = 132

TEST 1

0 × 11 =
1 × 11 =
2 × 11 =
3 × 11 =
4 × 11 =
5 × 11 =
6 × 11 =
7 × 11 =
8 × 11 =
9 × 11 =
10 × 11 =
11 × 11 =
12 × 11 =

Test yourself again here, and time how long it takes.

TEST 2

12 × 11   2 × 11   10 × 11   4 × 11

8 × 11   5 × 11   7 × 11   6 × 11   11 × 11

3 × 11   9 × 11   1 × 11   0 × 11

Time taken:

Multiplication table for 11

Try these questions about the 11 times table.

WARMING UP

1 How much are eleven 5p coins worth?

2 How many sides on 11 hexagons?

3 Find the product of 11 and 11.

4 How much do three £11 books cost?

5 What is the total weight of eleven 10 g weights?

6 Multiply 9 by 11.

7 What is eleven times zero?

8 There are 11 players in each football team. How many players are there in 8 teams?

9 Find 4 groups of 11.

10 What are twelve elevens?

GETTING HOTTER

11 How much change from £150 would you get if you bought eleven DVDs costing £12 each?

12 Jake can jog at a speed of 11 kilometres per hour. How far can he jog in 2 hours at this speed?

13 Amla is saving to buy a games console costing £95. She has saved £7 each week for 11 weeks. How much more money does she need to buy the console?

BURN IT UP!

14 At a school fun day, how much will five raffle tickets cost, if eleven tickets cost £1.21?

15 Find the difference between 11 × 9 and 2 × 11.

How did I do?

Division facts for 11

Division is the opposite of multiplication. $7 \times 11 = 77 \longrightarrow 77 \div 11 = 7$

Write a division question for each multiplication question.

$0 \times 11 = 0 \longrightarrow 0 \div 11 = 0$	$7 \times 11 = \quad\longrightarrow$
$1 \times 11 = 11 \longrightarrow 11 \div 11 = 1$	$8 \times 11 = \quad\longrightarrow$
$2 \times 11 = 22 \longrightarrow 22 \div 11 =$	$9 \times 11 = \quad\longrightarrow$
$3 \times 11 = 33 \longrightarrow$	$10 \times 11 = \quad\longrightarrow$
$4 \times 11 = 44 \longrightarrow$	$11 \times 11 = \quad\longrightarrow$
$5 \times 11 = 55 \longrightarrow$	$12 \times 11 = \quad\longrightarrow$
$6 \times 11 = 66 \longrightarrow$	

Now divide each of these numbers by 11 as quickly as you can. Time yourself.

TEST 2

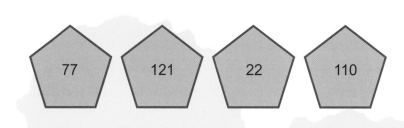

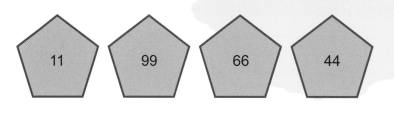

Time taken:

Division facts for 11

Remember your division facts for 11 to help you answer these.

WARMING UP

1   88 children are put into 11 teams. How many are in each team? ....

2   How many elevens are in 44? ....

3   Share 121 between 11. ....

4   How many 11p sweets can you buy with eight 10p coins? ....

5   What is one-eleventh of 66? ....

6   110 players. How many teams of 11? ....

7   Divide 132 by 11. ....

8   What is zero divided by 11? ....

9   What is the remainder when 50 is divided by 11? ....

GETTING HOTTER

10   A baker makes trays of cupcakes with 12 cakes on each tray. He bakes 132 cupcakes. How many trays does he make? ....

11   At an internet café, it costs 11p per minute to go online. For how long could you be online with £1.10? ....

12   Divide 121 by 11 and then divide the answer by 11. What do you get?

....

BURN IT UP!

13   Table-tennis balls cost £11 for a pack of 20. How many balls could you buy with £33? ....

14   Mr Philpot buys an £11 bag of dog food each month for his dog, Jess. In November, he gets two bags for the price of one, which is enough for two months. How much does he pay for dog food this year? ....

How did I do?

 ☐   ☐   ☐

Multiplication table for 12

Here is a table showing each number in the top row multiplied by 12.

0	1	2	3	4	5	6	7	8	9	10	11	12
0	12	24	36	48	60	72	84	96	108	120	132	144

Look at the numbers in the table, then cover it.

Fill in the table below by multiplying each number by 12.

0	1	2	3	4	5	6	7	8	9	10	11	12

Test yourself again and time how long it takes.

12 × 12 =		10 × 12 =		4 × 12 =
	7 × 12 =		2 × 12 =	
6 × 12 =		9 × 12 =		0 × 12 =
	11 × 12 =		1 × 12 =	
5 × 12 =		3 × 12 =		8 × 12 =

Time taken:

18

Multiplication table for 12

Use your knowledge of the 12 times table to answer these questions.

WARMING UP

1. How much are twelve 5p coins worth? ....

2. How many months in 9 years? ....

3. Find the product of 11 and 12. ....

4. Kim saves £10 each month. How much does she save in one year? ....

5. There are twelve bottles in a crate. How many bottles in 6 crates? ....

6. Multiply 7 by 12. ....

7. Multiply (4 × 2) by 12. ....

8. How many twelfths in 3 wholes? ....

9. What is 12 squared? ....

GETTING HOTTER

10. The school hall has a length of 12 m and a width of 7 m. What is its area?

    ....

11. A packet contains 12 cookies. For a school fair, a teacher buys eight packets of cookies. How many cookies are left after 50 of them have been eaten? ....

BURN IT UP!

12. Five sweets have a total mass of 12 g. What is the mass of 25 of the same sweets? ....

13. How much greater than 9 × 12 is 12 × 11? ....

14. Is each statement true or false? ....

    • Multiplying by 12 is the same as multiplying by 6 and then doubling.

      ....

    • Multiplying by 12 is the same as multiplying by 3 and then doubling and doubling again. ....

How did I do?

 ☐   ☐   ☐

Division facts for 12

Look at the division facts below, cover them up, then test yourself.

0 ÷ 12 = 0
12 ÷ 12 = 1
24 ÷ 12 = 2
36 ÷ 12 = 3
48 ÷ 12 = 4
60 ÷ 12 = 5
72 ÷ 12 = 6
84 ÷ 12 = 7
96 ÷ 12 = 8
108 ÷ 12 = 9
120 ÷ 12 = 10
132 ÷ 12 = 11
144 ÷ 12 = 12

TEST 1

0 ÷ 12 =
12 ÷ 12 =
24 ÷ 12 =
36 ÷ 12 =
48 ÷ 12 =
60 ÷ 12 =
72 ÷ 12 =
84 ÷ 12 =
96 ÷ 12 =
108 ÷ 12 =
120 ÷ 12 =
132 ÷ 12 =
144 ÷ 12 =

Divide each number by 12. Time yourself.

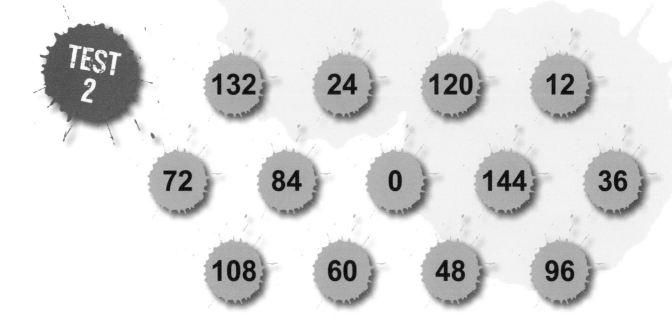

TEST 2

132   24   120   12

72   84   0   144   36

108   60   48   96

Time taken:

Division facts for 12

Use the division facts for 12 to help you answer these questions.

WARMING UP

1   Divide 132 by 12. ....

2   How many twelves make 120? ....

3   If 72 children get into teams of 12, how many teams are there? ....

4   Alex has 12 times as much money as Ella. Alex has £96. How much has Ella? ....

5   Share 48 sweets between 12. ....

6   What is one-twelfth of 84? ....

7   When 108 is divided by 12, what is the answer? ....

8   How long will it take to travel a distance of 60 km going at 12 km per hour? ....

9   A number squared is 144. What is the number? ....

GETTING HOTTER

10   A dodecagon (a polygon with 12 sides) has a perimeter of 120 cm. If all its sides are the same length, what is the length of each side? ....

11   How much change is left from £50 if David buys as many £12 pizzas as he can? ....

12   At a sports tournament, 132 players get into 12 equal teams. How many players are in each team? ....

BURN IT UP!

13   How many times larger is 72 ÷ 12 than 24 ÷ 12? ....

14   If 11 chews cost £1.32, what do 7 chews cost? ....

15   Lia saves the same amount each month to buy a mobile phone that costs £98. By the end of the year, she only needs £2 more. How much did she save each month? ....

How did I do?   ☐   ☐   ☐

Mixed multiplication practice (7 and 9)

The orange rods are 7 cubes long and the blue rods are 9 cubes long. Write a multiplication fact for each row of rods. Two have been done for you.

3 × 7 = 21

5 × 9 = 45

....

....

....

....

....

....

....

....

Complete these multiplications. Time yourself.

9 × 9 =	7 × 7 =	3 × 7 =
5 × 7 =	12 × 9 =	8 × 7 =
11 × 7 =	8 × 9 =	3 × 9 =
0 × 7 =	4 × 9 =	9 × 7 =
12 × 7 =	11 × 9 =	6 × 9 =

Time taken:

Mixed multiplication practice (7 and 9)

Use your knowledge of the 7 and 9 times tables to answer these questions.

WARMING UP

1   What is the weight altogether of four 9 g weights and three 7 g weights?

2   What is the total of 3 × 7 and 11 × 9? ....

3   How many sevens are the same as seven nines? ....

4   Find the difference between 11 × 9 and 6 × 7. ....

5   What is 3 × 3 × 7? ....

6   Which has more sides – seven squares or nine triangles? ....

7   Multiply zero by nine and multiply the answer by seven. ....

8   What is (12 × 9) – (8 × 7)? ....

GETTING HOTTER

9   A shop sells colour ink cartridges at £9 each and black ink cartridges at £7 each. How much do 6 colour cartridges and 4 black cartridges cost?

10   At a school fête, calendars are sold for £9 each and diaries for £7 each. How much did the school get if it sold 12 calendars and 9 diaries? ....

BURN IT UP!

11   Subtract the number of days in 5 weeks from the number of months in 9 years. ....

12   A hexagon has sides that are 7 cm long. A square has sides that are 9 cm long. Which shape has the longer perimeter and by how much?

13   Answer each question:

    1 × 7 × 7 × 2 ....   7 × 9 × 10 ....

    90 × 90 ....   7 × 7 × 9 × 9 × 9 × 0 ....

How did I do?

Mixed multiplication practice (11 and 12)

The turquoise rods are 11 cubes long and the red rods are 12 cubes long. Write a multiplication fact for each row of rods. Two have been done for you.

TEST 1

3 × 11 = 33

5 × 12 = 60

....

....

....

....

....

....

....

....

Complete this table. Time yourself.

TEST 2

×	11	12
6		
8		
4		
11		
7		
12		
9		

Time taken:

Mixed multiplication practice (11 and 12)

Use the multiplication facts to help you solve these problems.

WARMING UP

1 What is (11 × 12) + (3 × 11)? ....

2 What is the area of a square with sides of 12 cm? ....

3 Multiply twelve by eight by one. What is the answer? ....

4 Find the difference between 7 × 12 and 7 × 11. ....

5 Add 7 × 11 and 9 × 12. ....

6 Add the product of 11 and 12 to the product of 2 and 11. ....

7 Jo has £7. Kim has eleven times as much. How much does Kim have?

....

8 How many more are six elevens than five twelves? ....

GETTING HOTTER

9 A phone company charges 11p per minute for evening calls and 12p per minute for daytime calls. How much do 8 minutes of evening calls plus 12 minutes of daytime calls cost altogether? ....

10 A box has 12 milk chocolates and 11 dark chocolates. How many chocolates are there altogether in 9 boxes? ....

BURN IT UP!

11 Squaring a number means multiplying it by itself. What is 11 squared plus 12 squared? ....

12 If 9 × 11 = 99 and 10 × 11 = 110, what does 19 × 11 equal? ....

13 If 11 × 12 = 132 and 10 × 12 = 120, what does 21 × 12 equal? ....

How did I do?

 ☐   ☐   ☐

Mixed division practice (7 and 9)

Finding one-seventh, $\frac{1}{7}$, is the same as dividing by 7. Finding one-ninth, $\frac{1}{9}$, is the same as dividing by 9. Write the value of each:

TEST 1

One-seventh of 70 _____

$\frac{1}{7}$ of 63 _____

One-seventh of 84 _____

One-seventh of 77 _____

One-ninth of 72 _____

$\frac{1}{7}$ of 42 _____

One-ninth of 36 _____

One-seventh of 35 _____

One-ninth of 99 _____

$\frac{1}{9}$ of 81 _____

$\frac{1}{9}$ of 108 _____

$\frac{1}{7}$ of 56 _____

$\frac{1}{9}$ of 54 _____

One-seventh of 49 _____

$\frac{1}{9}$ of 63 _____

Answer these questions as quickly as you can. Time yourself.

TEST 2

27 ÷ 9 =	21 ÷ 7 =
7 ÷ 7 =	36 ÷ 9 =
108 ÷ 9 =	35 ÷ 7 =
28 ÷ 7 =	72 ÷ 9 =
18 ÷ 9 =	21 ÷ 7 =
63 ÷ 7 =	99 ÷ 9 =
54 ÷ 9 =	42 ÷ 7 =
0 ÷ 7 =	81 ÷ 9 =
90 ÷ 9 =	49 ÷ 7 =
84 ÷ 7 =	63 ÷ 9 =
9 ÷ 9 =	77 ÷ 7 =
14 ÷ 7 =	0 ÷ 9 =
45 ÷ 9 =	70 ÷ 7 =

Time taken: _____

Mixed division practice (7 and 9)

Use your knowledge of the division facts from the 7 and 9 times tables to help you solve these.

WARMING UP

1   Divide 63 by 9 and divide the answer by 7. What do you get? _____

2   Which number, less than 100, is a multiple of 7 and 9? _____

3   A number squared is 49. What is the number? _____

4   Divide 72 by 9 and add the answer to 42 divided by 7. _____

5   How many £9 books cost £72? _____

6   Find the difference between 99 ÷ 9 and 84 ÷ 7. _____

7   What is the remainder when 32 is divided by 7? _____

8   How many weeks are the same as 84 days? _____

9   What is zero divided by nine? _____

GETTING HOTTER

10   Find the difference between $\frac{1}{7}$ of 84 and $\frac{1}{9}$ of 63. _____

11   James has 89 litres of oil. He can either fill as many 9-litre containers as he can and have some left over, or he can fill as many 7-litre containers as he can with some left over. What size containers should he use to have the least left over, and how many containers will he fill? _____

BURN IT UP!

12   If seven cups of coffee cost £28, how much do nine cups of coffee cost?

_____

13   Joe has a collection of pencils that are 7 cm and 9 cm long. If he puts 6 of the pencils touching end to end and the length of these pencils is exactly $\frac{1}{2}$ a metre, how many of the pencils are 9 cm long? _____

How did I do?

Mixed division practice (11 and 12)

Finding one-eleventh, $\frac{1}{11}$, is the same as dividing by 11. Finding one-twelfth, $\frac{1}{12}$, is the same as dividing by 12. Write the value of each:

TEST 1

One-eleventh of 99 ....

$\frac{1}{11}$ of 55 ....

One-eleventh of 11 ....

One-twelfth of 144 ....

$\frac{1}{12}$ of 60 ....

One-eleventh of 132 ....

One-twelfth of 108 ....

One-twelfth of 132 ....

One-twelfth of 48 ....

$\frac{1}{12}$ of 72 ....

$\frac{1}{12}$ of 96 ....

$\frac{1}{11}$ of 121 ....

One-twelfth of 36 ....

$\frac{1}{12}$ of 84 ....

$\frac{1}{11}$ of 110 ....

Answer these questions as quickly as you can. Time yourself.

TEST 2

77 ÷ 11 =	120 ÷ 12 =
24 ÷ 12 =	66 ÷ 11 =
55 ÷ 11 =	36 ÷ 12 =
12 ÷ 12 =	44 ÷ 11 =
11 ÷ 11 =	72 ÷ 12 =
84 ÷ 12 =	0 ÷ 11 =
88 ÷ 11 =	48 ÷ 12 =
60 ÷ 12 =	99 ÷ 11 =
132 ÷ 11 =	132 ÷ 12 =
96 ÷ 12 =	110 ÷ 11 =
121 ÷ 11 =	0 ÷ 12 =
108 ÷ 12 =	33 ÷ 11 =
22 ÷ 11 =	144 ÷ 12 =

Time taken:

Mixed division practice (11 and 12)

Can you solve these problems using the facts you know?

WARMING UP

1 Add (120 ÷ 12) to (88 ÷ 11). ....

2 How many less than one-eleventh of 121 is one-twelfth of 96? ....

3 How many 12p sweets can I buy with 84p? ....

4 How many twelves are the same as 12 elevens? ....

5 Divide 144 by 12 and divide the answer by 3. What do you get? ....

6 How many £12 T-shirts can I buy with three £20 notes? ....

7 Share 132 between 12 and divide the answer by 11. ....

8 What is the remainder when 80 is divided by 11? ....

GETTING HOTTER

9 A mobile phone contract charges 11p per minute plus 12p per call. Katy paid 90p for making two calls. For how many minutes in total did the two calls last? ....

10 If four cups of tea cost £12, how much do eleven cups of tea cost?

....

BURN IT UP!

11 Joe has a collection of pencils that are 11 cm and 12 cm long. If he puts 9 of the pencils touching end to end and the length of these pencils is 1 metre, how many of the pencils are 12 cm long?

12 The equals sign shows that what is on one side is equal to what is on the other side. For example: 96 ÷ 12 = 88 ÷ 11.

Fill in the missing numbers so that each statement is true.

24 ÷ [   ] = 22 ÷ 11   [   ] ÷ 12 = 55 ÷ 11

[   ] ÷ 12 = 77 ÷ 11   144 ÷ 12 = [   ] ÷ 11

How did I do?

 ☐   ☐   ☐

Mixed multiplication practice (7, 9, 11 and 12)

Each strip of stamps contains 7p, 9p, 11p or 12p stamps. How much is each strip worth?

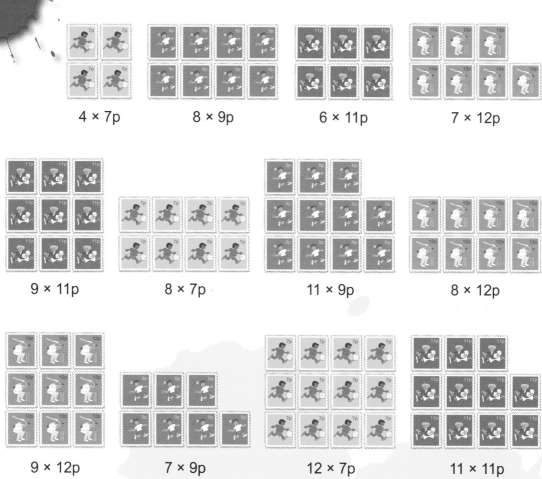

4 × 7p   8 × 9p   6 × 11p   7 × 12p

9 × 11p   8 × 7p   11 × 9p   8 × 12p

9 × 12p   7 × 9p   12 × 7p   11 × 11p

Multiply the number at the left of each row by the number at the top of each column to complete the table. Time yourself.

×	8	12	6	9	11
7					
9					
11					
12					

Time taken:

Mixed multiplication practice (7, 9, 11 and 12)

Use your knowledge of these times tables to answer these questions.

WARMING UP

1   How many nines are equal to three twelves? ....

2   Find the product of 9 and 12. ....

3   What is the fourth multiple of 9 plus the fourth multiple of 11? ....

4   Find the difference between 5 × 12 and 7 × 9. ....

5   Subtract 4 × 7 from 12 × 11. ....

6   Find the cost of six 9p sweets, three 11p sweets and ten 7p sweets.

   ....

7   Add 3 × 7, 8 × 9 and 12 × 12. ....

8   What is 7 squared plus 9 squared? ....

9   Find the total of 7 × 9 and 7 × 11 and halve the answer. ....

GETTING HOTTER

10 Two runners go out for a run. Shelly runs for 3 hours at 11 km per hour.
    Deena runs for 4 hours at 9 km per hour. Who runs further and by
    how much? ....

11 Jenny and Ben have the same amount of money. Jenny has seven £5
    notes and nine £2 coins. Ben has nine £5 notes and some £1 coins.
    How many £1 coins does he have? ....

BURN IT UP!

12 I'm thinking of a secret number. I multiply it by 9. I also multiply it by 11.
    When I add the two answers I get 220. What is my secret number? ....

13 I'm thinking of a secret number. I multiply it by 7. I also multiply it by 12.
    When I add the two answers I get 152. What is my secret number? ....

How did I do?

Mixed division practice (7, 9, 11 and 12)

For each multiple, show its factors by circling 7, 9, 11 or 12. Write underneath which multiple it is. The first one has been done for you.

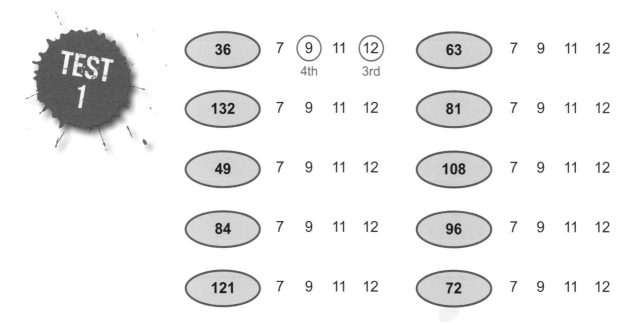

TEST 1

36	7 (9) 11 (12)	63	7 9 11 12
	4th 3rd		
132	7 9 11 12	81	7 9 11 12
49	7 9 11 12	108	7 9 11 12
84	7 9 11 12	96	7 9 11 12
121	7 9 11 12	72	7 9 11 12

Now write the remainder when each of these numbers is divided by 7, 9, 11 or 12. Time yourself.

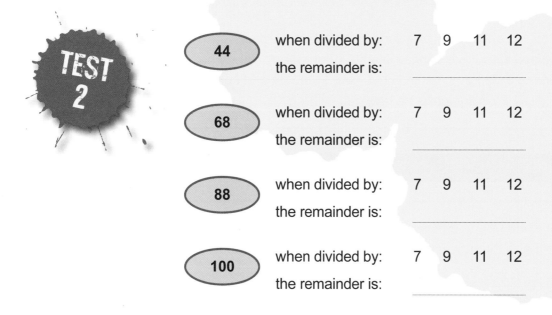

TEST 2

44 when divided by: 7   9   11   12
    the remainder is: ....

68 when divided by: 7   9   11   12
    the remainder is: ....

88 when divided by: 7   9   11   12
    the remainder is: ....

100 when divided by: 7   9   11   12
    the remainder is: ....

Time taken:

Mixed division practice (7, 9, 11 and 12)

Use division facts to help you solve these.

1   Divide 132 by 11 and the answer by 12. What number do you get? _____

2   How many groups of 9 in 108? _____

3   One-ninth of 72 is one-seventh of what number? _____

4   Find one-twelfth of 72 and multiply the answer by 9. _____

5   Add (144 ÷ 12) to (49 ÷ 7). _____

6   Add one-eleventh of 121 to one-ninth of 54. _____

7   How many twelves are the same as four nines? _____

8   Find the difference between 84 ÷ 12 and 56 ÷ 7. _____

9   What is zero divided by twelve multiplied by 11? _____

GETTING HOTTER

10 Each of the 11 pods of a Ferris wheel can hold 12 people. There are 111 people on the wheel, and 4 pods are full. The other 7 pods have an equal number of people in them. How many people are in each of these 7 pods?

_____

11 A customer buys some 9p stamps, two 11p stamps and three 12p stamps. He pays with a £2 coin and is given 34p change. How many 9p stamps did he buy? _____

BURN IT UP!

12 I'm thinking of a secret number between 50 and 70. When it is divided by 11, the remainder is 5. When it is divided by 12, the remainder is 0. What is the remainder when it is divided by 9? _____

13 I'm thinking of a secret number between 60 and 90. When it is divided by 11, the remainder is 9. When it is divided by 12, the remainder is 2. What is the remainder when it is divided by 9? _____

How did I do?

 ☐   ☐   ☐

Fill in the missing numbers in these multiplications. Time yourself.

9 × 9 = [   ]   [   ] × 7 = 84   9 × [   ] = 27

7 × [   ] = 28   9 × [   ] = 72   [   ] × 9 = 0

7 × 7 = [   ]   [   ] × 9 = 54   9 × [   ] = 99

[   ] × 9 = 108   10 × 9 = [   ]   [   ] × 7 = 77

7 × [   ] = 42   7 × [   ] = 56   4 × 9 = [   ]

This is a magic square. The three numbers in each row, column and diagonal add up to 15. Multiply each number in the square by 7 to create a new set of numbers. Time yourself.

2	7	6
9	5	1
4	3	8

14		

Is the new square a magic square? If so, what do the numbers add up to? ....

Time taken: [   ]

Problem solving (7 and 9 times tables)

WARMING UP

1   Add the fourth multiple of 9 to the ninth multiple of 7. ....

2   Write 4 tables facts from the 7 or 9 times table that have square-number answers. (A square number is a number multiplied by itself. For example: 1, 4, 9, 16, 25, 36, 49, 64, 81, 100…)

GETTING HOTTER

3   There are 7p stamps and 9p stamps. Which totals between 40p and 55p can be made with these stamps?
    For example: **41p** = 2 × 7p + 3 × 9p, **42p** = 6 × 7p, **43p** = 1 × 7p + 4 × 9p, **44p** = 5 × 7p + 1 × 9p

    ....

    ....

    Which totals cannot be made? ....

BURN IT UP!

4   Write the unit digit of each multiple of 7 from 7 to 84. What do you notice about the digits? ....

5   Write the unit digit of each multiple of 9 from 9 to 108. What do you notice about the digits? ....

6   Multiply adjacent blue numbers and write the answers in the spaces. (One has been done for you.) Find the total of the four answers. Which of these baubles has the highest total?

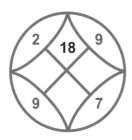

How did I do?

35

Problem solving (7 and 9 division facts)

Write a division fact for the 9 times table that gives each number on the clock.

TEST 1

Fill in the missing numbers in these divisions. Time yourself.

TEST 2

9 ÷ 9 = [   ]   [   ] ÷ 7 = 9   84 ÷ [   ] = 12

[   ] ÷ 7 = 7   [   ] ÷ 9 = 9   [   ] ÷ 7 = 0

21 ÷ 7 = [   ]   [   ] ÷ 9 = 6   108 ÷ [   ] = 12

[   ] ÷ 7 = 8   28 ÷ 7 = [   ]   [   ] ÷ 7 = 6

99 ÷ [   ] = 11   72 ÷ [   ] = 8   [   ] ÷ 9 = 5

Time taken:

Problem solving (7 and 9 division facts)

1 Write a word problem for each of these divisions:

$84 \div 7 = ?$ ....

$0 \div 9 = ?$ ....

$99 \div 9 = ?$ ....

2 Use these digit cards to make as many different division facts as you can. You can use each card as many times as you like, for example: $7 \div 3 = 21$, $9 \div 9 = 1$. Can you make 9 different division facts from the 7 and 9 times tables?

| 1 | 2 | 3 | 7 | 8 | 9 | ÷ | = |

3 This is a magic square. Arrange the remaining tiles into the grid so that the three answers in each row, column and diagonal add up to 15.

$36 \div 9$	$81 \div 9$	$14 \div 7$
	$45 \div 9$	
	$7 \div 7$	

$4 + 9 + 2 = 15$

$54 \div 9$

$56 \div 7$ $21 \div 7$ $49 \div 7$

How did I do?

37

Fill in the missing numbers in these multiplications. Time yourself.

11 × 12 = [   ]   [   ] × 11 = 11   11 × [   ] = 99

12 × [   ] = 120   9 × [   ] = 108   [   ] × 12 = 0

7 × 11 = [   ]   [   ] × 12 = 36   12 × [   ] = 60

[   ] × 12 = 12   3 × 11 = [   ]   [   ] × 12 = 84

12 × [   ] = 72   11 × [   ] = 110   8 × 12 = [   ]

This is a magic square. The three numbers in each row, column and diagonal add up to 15. Multiply each number in the square by 12 to create a new set of numbers. Time yourself.

4	9	2
3	5	7
8	1	6

48		

Is the new square a magic square? If so, what do the numbers add up to? _____

Time taken:

Problem solving (11 and 12 times tables)

WARMING UP

1 Add the third multiple of 11 to the ninth multiple of 12. _____

2 Write 3 tables facts from the 11 or 12 times table that have square-number answers. (A square number is a number multiplied by itself. For example: 1, 4, 9, 16, 25, 36, 49, 64, 81, 100, 121, 144…) _____

GETTING HOTTER

3 There are 11p stamps and 12p stamps. Which totals between 55p and 75p can be made with these stamps?
For example: **55p** = 5 × 11p, **56p** = 4 × 11 + 1 × 12p,
57p = 3 × 11p + 2 × 12p…

_____

_____

Which totals cannot be made? _____

BURN IT UP!

4 Write the answers to these questions in words, one letter in each box. Then write a multiplication or division question with the answer that reads downwards.

3 × 12

2 × 11

7 × 12

1 × 11

6 × 12

9 × 11

5 Make up your own puzzle like the one above.

How did I do?

39

Write a division fact for the 12 times table that gives each number on the clock.

TEST 1

Fill in the missing numbers in these divisions. Time yourself.

TEST 2

66 ÷ 11 = [   ]   [   ] ÷ 12 = 9   120 ÷ [   ] = 12

84 ÷ [   ] = 7   132 ÷ [   ] = 11   [   ] ÷ 11 = 0

48 ÷ 12 = [   ]   [   ] ÷ 11 = 9   [   ] ÷ 12 = 6

[   ] ÷ 12 = 5   96 ÷ 12 = [   ]   [   ] ÷ 12 = 12

121 ÷ [   ] = 11   108 ÷ [   ] = 12   [   ] ÷ 10 = 12

Time taken:

Problem solving (11 and 12 division facts)

1 Squaring a number means multiplying a number by itself. What is the sum of 11 squared and 12 squared? _____

2 What is the difference between 121 divided by 11 and 72 divided by 12?

_____

3 Place multiples of 11 and 12 that are less than 150 into this diagram.

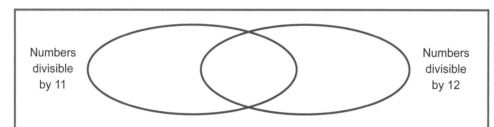

Numbers divisible by 11

Numbers divisible by 12

What number is in the middle section? _____

4 This is a magic square. Arrange the remaining tiles into the grid so that the three answers in each row, column and diagonal make a total of 15.

44 ÷ 11	108 ÷ 12	24 ÷ 12
	11 ÷ 11	

4 + 9 + 2 = 15

84 ÷ 12

55 ÷ 11

72 ÷ 12

33 ÷ 11

96 ÷ 12

How did I do?

  ☐   ☐   ☐

Problem solving (7, 9, 11 and 12 times tables)

How many times does the digit 3 appear in the answers to these questions?

TEST 1

| 3 × 12 | 5 × 7 | 6 × 9 |

| 11 × 7 | 8 × 9 | 3 × 11 |

| 7 × 9 | 8 × 7 | 12 × 9 |

| 12 × 12 | 7 × 7 | 4 × 9 |

Fill in the missing numbers in these divisions. Time yourself.

TEST 2

9 × 9 = [   ]   [   ] × 7 = 49   11 × [   ] = 121

12 × [   ] = 132   11 × [   ] = 44   [   ] × 7 = 7

0 × 9 = [   ]   7 × 9 = [   ]   12 × [   ] = 144

8 × 7 = [   ]   9 × 6 = [   ]   [   ] × 7 = 28

12 × [   ] = 48   11 × [   ] = 55   12 × 8 = [   ]

Time taken:

Problem solving (7, 9, 11 and 12 times tables)

1 Answer these questions:

11 × 11 × 2 = ... 7 × 7 × 2 = ... 9 × 9 × 2 = ... 9 × 12 × 11 × 0 = ...

2 What is the ninth multiple of 9 plus the eleventh multiple of 11? ....

3 Fill in the missing digits to make each answer correct.

Can you complete the second grid in the same way?

Make up more of your own puzzles.

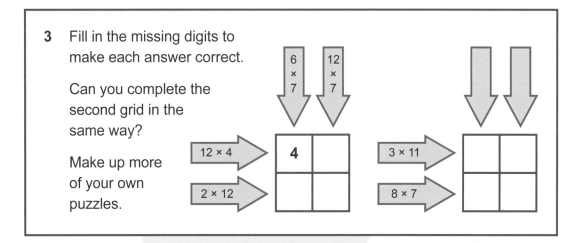

4 Use these digit cards to make as many different tables facts as you can. You can use each card as many times as you like, for example: 11 × 11 = 121, 4 × 7 = 28. Can you make more than 12 different facts from your 7, 9, 11 and 12 times tables?

| 1 | 2 | 4 | 7 | 8 | 9 | × | = |

....

....

....

How did I do?

 ☐   ☐   ☐

Problem solving (7, 9, 11 and 12 division facts)

Find sets of questions with the same answer. Colour each set the same colour.

TEST 1

84 ÷ 12	0 ÷ 12	70 ÷ 7	99 ÷ 9	18 ÷ 9
132 ÷ 11	49 ÷ 7	121 ÷ 11	90 ÷ 9	120 ÷ 12
70 ÷ 7	88 ÷ 11	63 ÷ 9	11 ÷ 11	0 ÷ 9
60 ÷ 12	7 ÷ 7	55 ÷ 11	28 ÷ 7	72 ÷ 12
72 ÷ 9	24 ÷ 12	33 ÷ 11	21 ÷ 7	110 ÷ 11
27 ÷ 9	48 ÷ 12	66 ÷ 11	108 ÷ 9	144 ÷ 12

Fill in the missing numbers in these divisions. Time yourself.

TEST 2

90 ÷ 9 = [   ]   [   ] ÷ 12 = 7   144 ÷ [   ] = 12

77 ÷ 11 = [   ]   [   ] ÷ 9 = 7   [   ] ÷ 7 = 7

[   ] ÷ 9 = 0   72 ÷ 12 = [   ]   [   ] ÷ 11 = 12

45 ÷ [   ] = 9   96 ÷ [   ] = 12   [   ] ÷ 7 = 8

Time taken:

44

Problem solving (7, 9, 11 and 12 division facts)

WARMING UP

1 Kim spent £1.10 on 9p, 11p and 12p stamps. She bought twice as many 11p stamps as 9p stamps. If she bought four 12p stamps, what other stamps did she buy? ....

2 Find the total of the ninth multiple of 9, the fourth multiple of 11, the second multiple of 7 and the seventh multiple of 12.

GETTING HOTTER

3 Use these digit cards to make as many different division facts as you can. You can use each card as many times as you like, for example: 28 ÷ 7 = 4, 99 ÷ 9 = 11. Can you make more than 12 different division facts related to the 7, 9, 11 and 12 times tables?

| 1 | 2 | 4 | 7 | 8 | 9 | ÷ | = |

....

....

BURN IT UP!

4 Use the clues to fill in this puzzle. Write divisions or multiplications for the missing clues.

Across
1 99 ÷ 9
2 84 ÷ 7
3 5 × 12
4 8 × 7
6 ....
7 121 ÷ 11
8 6 × 12

Down
1 144 ÷ 12
2 110 ÷ 11
3 ....
4 6 × 9
5 3 × 7
6 4 × 7
7 108 ÷ 9

How did I do?

45

Hints and tips

When learning your times tables and related division facts there are some useful things to remember:

- The order of the numbers in a multiplication question doesn't matter as the answer will be the same, for example 6 × 2 = 12 and 2 × 6 = 12. It means that you learn two facts for the price of one!

- If you know multiplication facts then you also know related division facts. If you know that 6 × 2 = 12 and 2 × 6 = 12 then you also know that 12 ÷ 2 = 6 and 12 ÷ 6 = 2. This means that you actually learn four facts for the price of one!

- You might find it easier to learn the facts in order at first, but make sure that you begin to learn to answer questions in any order.

- Look for patterns in the numbers to help you check your answers. For example: the answers for the facts in the 2, 4, 6 and 8 times tables are always even; the answers to the 10 times table end in 0; the answers to the 5 times table end in 0 or 5; the digits of the answers to the 9 times table always add up to 9 or 18 and so on.

- As you learn a table there will always be some facts that you find more difficult to remember than others. Focus on learning these facts using the tips below.

Try these different approaches:

- Say facts aloud using a range of voices: high or low voices, whispering, croaking, singing, shouting, speaking with the voice of a cat, snake, worm, monster and so on!

- Write questions onto small pieces of paper or card and the answers on the other side. Use them to test yourself at different times. Put them on the fridge, on a noticeboard or even on your stairs. Each time you see the card try to remember the answer.

- Draw pictures for the questions you find most difficult, such as drawing a picture of 5 rows of 9 flowers to help you with the question 'How many 5s in 45?'

- Write out facts in words rather than just using numbers. For example: for 24 ÷ 2, write 'Twenty-four divided by two is twelve'.

- Make up rhymes and songs to help you learn facts that you find difficult to remember, such as 'Clap, bang, thump the floor because 8 times 8 is sixty-four' or 'Turn off the telly and touch the screen as 4 lots of 4 equals sixteen'. Use movements and gestures in the rhymes, as this can also help you to remember them more easily.

Answers

Multiplication table for 7 (pages 6–7)

Test 1 49, 35, 7, 70, 63, 77, 42, 84, 28, 14, 56, 21

Test 2 77, 84, 63, 21
7, 49, 63, 0
84, 70, 0, 42
14, 56, 28, 35

1 49	**2** 63	**3** 84
4 21	**5** 28	**6** 77
7 42	**8** 0	**9** £84
10 7	**11** 56	**12** 35 km
13 14	**14** 21 cm	

Division facts for 7 (pages 8–9)

Test 1 0, 1, 2, 3, 4, 5, 6, 7, 8, 9, 10, 11, 12

Test 2 7, 5, 11
9, 2, 1
3, 10, 12
8, 6, 4

1 6	**2** 0	**3** 5
4 7	**5** 4	**6** 10
7 11	**8** 0	**9** £51
10 84 kg	**11** 3	

12 False – only if it is a multiple of 7.
13 True

Multiplication table for 9 (pages 10–11)

Test 1 9, 18, 27, 36, 45, 54, 63, 72, 81, 90, 99, 108

Test 2 0, 99, 27, 90, 9
36, 81, 54, 108, 0, 45
108, 63, 18, 54, 72

1 54	**2** 18	**3** 90p
4 72	**5** 63	**6** 108
7 45 kg	**8** 36	**9** 99
10 19	**11** 36	**12** 63 cm²
13 117, 171, 144	**14** 5	

Division facts for 9 (pages 12–13)

Test 1 11, 10, 0, 1, 9, 3, 7, 5, 4, 6, 8, 12

Test 2 2, 12, 7, 5
8, 3, 1, 10, 0
9, 4, 6, 11

1 3	**2** 8	**3** 1
4 7	**5** 4	**6** 11
7 6	**8** 12	**9** 8
10 11 tickets, £1 change	**11** 7	
12 4	**13** 9 litres, £6.30	

Multiplication table for 11 (pages 14–15)

Test 1 0, 11, 22, 33, 44, 55, 66, 77, 88, 99, 110, 121, 132

Test 2 132, 22, 110, 44
88, 55, 77, 66, 121
33, 99, 11, 0

1 55p	**2** 66	**3** 121
4 £33	**5** 110 g	**6** 99
7 0	**8** 88	**9** 44
10 132	**11** £18	**12** 22 km
13 £18	**14** 55p	**15** 77

Division facts for 11 (pages 16–17)

Test 1 22 ÷ 11 = 2, 33 ÷ 11 = 3, 44 ÷ 11 = 4,
55 ÷ 11 = 5, 66 ÷ 11 = 6, 77 ÷ 11 = 7,
88 ÷ 11 = 8, 99 ÷ 11 = 9, 110 ÷ 11 = 10,
121 ÷ 11 = 11, 132 ÷ 11 = 12

Test 2 7, 11, 2, 10
3, 8, 5, 12, 0
1, 9, 6, 4

1 8	**2** 4	**3** 11
4 7 (with 3p change)		**5** 6
6 10	**7** 12	**8** 0
9 6	**10** 11	**11** 10 minutes
12 1	**13** 60	**14** £121

Multiplication table for 12 (pages 18–19)

Test 1 0, 12, 24, 36, 48, 60, 72, 84, 96, 108,
120, 132, 144

Test 2 144, 120, 48
84, 24
72, 108, 0
132, 12
60, 36, 96

1 60p	**2** 108	**3** 132
4 £120	**5** 72	**6** 84
7 96	**8** 36	**9** 144
10 84 m²	**11** 46	**12** 60 g
13 24	**14** True, true	

Division facts for 12 (pages 20–21)

Test 1 0, 1, 2, 3, 4, 5, 6, 7, 8, 9, 10, 11, 12

Test 2 11, 2, 10, 1
6, 7, 0, 12, 3
9, 5, 4, 8

1 11	**2** 10	**3** 6
4 £8	**5** 4	**6** 7
7 9	**8** 5 hours	**9** 12
10 10 cm	**11** £2	**12** 11
13 3	**14** 84p	**15** £8

Mixed multiplication practice (7 and 9) (pages 22–23)

Test 1 6 × 7 = 42, 7 × 9 = 63, 8 × 7 = 56,
4 × 9 = 36, 5 × 7 = 35, 6 × 9 = 54,
7 × 7 = 49, 3 × 9 = 27

Test 2 81, 49, 21
35, 108, 56
77, 72, 27
0, 36, 63
84, 99, 54

1 57 g	**2** 120	**3** 9
4 57	**5** 63	**6** 7 squares
7 0	**8** 52	**9** £82
10 £171	**11** 73	

12 Hexagon by 6 cm.
13 98, 630, 8100, 0

Mixed multiplication practice (11 and 12) (pages 24–25)

Test 1 5 × 11 = 55, 3 × 12 = 36, 4 × 11 = 44,
6 × 12 = 72, 7 × 11 = 77, 2 × 12 = 24,
6 × 11 = 66, 4 × 12 = 48

Test 2 66, 72
88, 96
44, 48
121, 132
77, 84
132, 144
99, 108

1 165	**2** 144 cm²	**3** 96
4 7	**5** 185	**6** 154
7 £77	**8** 6	**9** £2.32
10 207	**11** 121 + 144 = 265	
12 209	**13** 252	

Mixed division practice (7 and 9) (pages 26–27)

Test 1 10, 11
9, 9
12, 12
11, 8
8, 6
6, 7
4, 7
5

Test 2 3, 1, 12, 4, 2, 9, 6, 0, 10, 12, 1, 2, 5
3, 4, 5, 8, 3, 11, 6, 9, 7, 7, 11, 0, 10

1 1	**2** 63	**3** 7
4 14	**5** 8	**6** 1
7 4	**8** 12	**9** 0
10 5		

11 12 × 7-litre cans with 5 litres left over
12 £36 **13** 4 × 9 cm (and 2 × 7 cm)

Mixed division practice (11 and 12) (pages 28–29)

Test 1 9, 4
5, 6
1, 8
12, 11
5, 3
12, 7
9, 10
11

Test 2 7, 2, 5, 1, 1, 7, 8, 5, 12, 8, 11, 9, 2
10, 6, 3, 4, 6, 0, 4, 9, 11, 10, 0, 3, 12

1 18	**2** 3	**3** 7
4 11	**5** 4	**6** 5
7 1	**8** 3	**9** 6 minutes
10 £33	**11** 1 × 12 cm (and 8 × 11 cm)	
12 12, 60 84, 132		

Mixed multiplication practice (7, 9, 11 and 12) (pages 30–31)

Test 1 28p, 72p, 66p, 84p = £2.50
99p, 56p, 99p, 96p = £3.50
£1.08, 63p, 84p, £1.21 = £3.76

Test 2 56, 84, 42, 63, 77
72, 108, 54, 81, 99
88, 132, 66, 99, 121
96, 144, 72, 108, 132

Answers

1 4 **2** 108 **3** 80
4 3 **5** 104 **6** £1.57
7 237 **8** 130 **9** 70
10 Deena runs 3 km more **11** 8
12 11 **13** 8

Mixed division practice (7, 9, 11 and 12) (pages 32–33)

Test 1 11: 12th and 12: 11th
7: 7th
7: 12th and 12: 7th
11: 11th
7: 9th and 9: 7th
9: 9th
9: 12th and 12: 9th
12: 8th
9: 8th and 12: 6th

Test 2 2, 8, 0, 8
5, 5, 2, 8
4, 7, 0, 4
2, 1, 1, 4

1 1 **2** 12 **3** 56
4 54 **5** 19 **6** 17
7 3 **8** 1 **9** 0
10 9 **11** 12
12 6 (the secret number is 60)
13 5 (the secret number is 86)

Problem solving (7 and 9 times tables) (pages 34–35)

Test 1 81, 12, 3
4, 8, 0
49, 6, 11
12, 90, 11
6, 8, 36

Test 2 14, 49, 42
63, 35, 7
28, 21, 56
Yes, totals add to 105.

1 99
2 $1 \times 9 = 9$, $4 \times 9 = 36$, $7 \times 7 = 49$,
$9 \times 9 = 81$
3 45p = 5 × 9p, 46p = 4 × 7p + 2 × 9p,
48p = 3 × 7p + 3 × 9p, 49p = 7 × 7p,
50p = 2 × 7p + 4 × 9p, 51p = 6 × 7p + 1 × 9p,
52p = 1 × 7p + 5 × 9p, 53p = 5 × 7p + 2 × 9p,
54p = 6 × 9p, 55p = 4 × 7p + 3 × 9p
40p and 47p cannot be made.
4 7, 4, 1, 8, 5, 2, 9, 6, 3, 0, 7, 4...
All the digits occur and then begin to repeat.
5 9, 8, 7, 6, 5, 4, 3, 2, 1, 0, 9, 8...
The pattern goes down in ones and repeats.
6 18 + 18 + 63 + 63 = 162,
77 + 99 + 81 + 63 = 320,
35 + 45 + 63 + 49 = 192.

Problem solving (7 and 9 division facts) (pages 36–37)

Test 1 $9 \div 9 = 1$, $18 \div 9 = 2$, $27 \div 9 = 3$,
$36 \div 9 = 4$, $45 \div 9 = 5$, $54 \div 9 = 6$,
$63 \div 9 = 7$, $72 \div 9 = 8$, $81 \div 9 = 9$,
$90 \div 9 = 10$, $99 \div 9 = 11$, $108 \div 9 = 12$

Test 2 1, 63, 7
49, 81, 0
3, 54, 9
56, 4, 42
9, 9, 45

1 Answers will vary
2 Possible answers include:
$7 \div 7 = 1$, $21 \div 7 = 3$, $77 \div 7 = 11$,
$9 \div 9 = 1$, $18 \div 9 = 2$, $27 \div 9 = 3$,
$72 \div 9 = 8$, $81 \div 9 = 9$, $99 \div 9 = 11$
3 Middle: $21 \div 7$, $49 \div 7$
Bottom: $56 \div 7$, $54 \div 9$

Problem solving (11 and 12 times tables) (pages 38–39)

Test 1 132, 1, 9
10, 12, 0
77, 3, 5
1, 33, 7
6, 10, 96

Test 2 48, 108, 24
36, 60, 84
96, 12, 72
Yes, totals add up to 180.

1 141
2 $11 \times 11 = 121$, $3 \times 12 = 36$, $12 \times 12 = 144$
3 58p = 2 × 11p + 3 × 12p, 59p = 1 × 11p + 4 × 12p,
60p = 5 × 12p, 66p = 6 × 11p,
67p = 5 × 11p + 1 × 12p, 68p = 4 × 11p + 2 × 12p,
69p = 3 × 11p + 3 × 12p, 70p = 2 × 11p + 4 × 12p,
71p = 1 × 11p + 5 × 12p, 72p = 6 × 12p
61p, 62p, 63p, 64p, 65p, 73p, 74p and 75p
cannot be made.
4 thirtysix, twentytwo, eightyfour, eleven,
seventytwo, ninetynine. The word down
spells twelve.
5 Answers will vary

Problem solving (11 and 12 division facts) (pages 40–41)

Test 1 $12 \div 12 = 1$, $24 \div 12 = 2$,
$36 \div 12 = 3$, $48 \div 12 = 4$,
$60 \div 12 = 5$, $72 \div 12 = 6$,
$84 \div 12 = 7$, $96 \div 12 = 8$,
$108 \div 12 = 9$, $120 \div 12 = 10$,
$132 \div 12 = 11$, $144 \div 12 = 12$

Test 2 6, 108, 10
12, 12, 0
4, 99, 72
60, 8, 144
11, 9, 120

1 265 **2** 5
3 The number in the overlapping section is 132.
4 **Middle:** $33 \div 11$, $55 \div 11$, $84 \div 12$
Bottom: $96 \div 12$, $72 \div 12$

Problem solving (7, 9, 11 and 12 times tables) (pages 42–43)

Test 1 36, 35, 54
77, 72, 33
63, 56, 108
144, 49, 36
The digit 3 appears 6 times.

Test 2 81, 7, 11
11, 4, 1
0, 63, 12
56, 54, 4
4, 5, 96

1 242, 98
162, 0
2 202
3 1st grid top row **48**, bottom row **24**.
2nd grid top row **33**, bottom row **56**.
1st arrow **7 × 5**.
2nd arrow **12 × 3** or **9 × 4**.
4 There are more than 20 possible solutions.

Problem solving (7, 9, 11 and 12 division facts) (pages 44–45)

Test 1

84 ÷ 12	0 ÷ 12	70 ÷ 7	99 ÷ 9	18 ÷ 9
132 ÷ 11	49 ÷ 7	121 ÷ 11	90 ÷ 9	120 ÷ 12
70 ÷ 7	88 ÷ 11	63 ÷ 9	11 ÷ 11	0 ÷ 9
60 ÷ 12	7 ÷ 7	55 ÷ 11	28 ÷ 7	72 ÷ 12
72 ÷ 9	24 ÷ 12	33 ÷ 11	21 ÷ 7	110 ÷ 11
27 ÷ 9	48 ÷ 12	66 ÷ 11	108 ÷ 9	144 ÷ 12

Test 2 10, 84, 12
7, 63, 49
0, 6, 132
5, 8, 56

1 2 × 9p and 4 × 11p
2 223
3 There are more than 20 possible solutions.
4 Across: 1. 11, 2. 12, 3. 60, 4. 56, 6. 24, 7. 11,
8. 72
Down: 1. 12, 2. 10, 3. 66, 4. 54, 5. 21, 6. 28,
7. 12
6 across clue: 2 × 12; 3 down clue: 6 × 11